First World War
and Army of Occupation
War Diary
France, Belgium and Germany

41 DIVISION
Divisional Troops
Royal Army Veterinary Corps
52 Mobile Veterinary Section
2 March 1918 - 29 October 1919

WO95/2630/5

The Naval & Military Press Ltd
www.nmarchive.com
Published in association with The National Archives

Published by

The Naval & Military Press Ltd

Unit 10 Ridgewood Industrial Park,

Uckfield, East Sussex,

TN22 5QE England

Tel: +44 (0) 1825 749494

www.naval-military-press.com

www.nmarchive.com

This diary has been reprinted in facsimile from the original. Any imperfections are inevitably reproduced and the quality may fall short of modern type and cartographic standards.

© **Crown Copyright**
Images reproduced by permission of The National Archives, London, England, 2015.

Contents

Document type	Place/Title	Date From	Date To
Heading	WO95/2630/5 Mar 1918-Oct 1919 52 Mobile Veterinary Section		
Heading	52nd Mobile Vety Secn. May 1916 1917 Oct 1918 Mar 1919 Oct		
War Diary	Camposampiero	02/03/1918	24/03/1918
War Diary	Puisieux	25/03/1918	30/03/1918
War Diary	Authie	01/04/1918	01/04/1918
War Diary	Famechon	02/04/1918	03/04/1918
War Diary	Petit Houvin	04/04/1918	04/04/1918
War Diary	K.7.c.5.4.	07/04/1918	07/04/1918
War Diary	K.5.d.8.7.	08/04/1918	08/04/1918
War Diary	Sheet.27. K.5d.8.7.	09/04/1918	10/04/1918
War Diary	Sheet: 28. S.5.b.7.6.	11/04/1918	21/04/1918
War Diary	A.28.d.9.4. Sheet: 28.	22/04/1918	27/04/1918
War Diary	F.28.b.7.1. Sheet: 27.	28/04/1918	01/05/1918
War Diary	F.27.a.2.9.	02/05/1918	14/05/1918
War Diary	Sheet 27. F.27.a.2.9.	16/05/1918	30/05/1918
War Diary	F.27.a.2.9. Sheet 27.	01/06/1918	04/06/1918
War Diary	Kinderbelck	06/06/1918	10/06/1918
War Diary	Eperlecques.	13/06/1918	28/06/1918
War Diary	Map 5a. L.15.b.9.2.	01/07/1918	01/07/1918
War Diary	Sheet 27. K.21.d.7.3.	02/07/1918	10/07/1918
War Diary	K.21.d.7.3.	10/07/1918	12/07/1918
War Diary	K.27.d.9.4.	14/07/1918	19/07/1918
War Diary	K.27.d.9.4. Sheet 27.	20/07/1918	28/07/1918
War Diary	Sheet 27. K.27.d.9.7.	28/07/1918	31/07/1918
War Diary	Sheet: 27. K.27.c.9.7.	01/08/1918	12/08/1918
War Diary	K.27.d9.7.	13/08/1918	20/08/1918
War Diary	K.27.d.9.7. Sheet 27.	21/08/1918	31/08/1918
War Diary	Wizernes.	01/09/1918	03/09/1918
War Diary	Sheet 27.Z.13.d.25.	04/09/1918	08/09/1918
War Diary	Sheet 28.G.26.a.	01/09/1918	15/09/1918
War Diary	Sheet 27.Z:28.c.2.7.	17/09/1918	21/09/1918
War Diary	L.28.c.2.7. Sheet: 28.	23/09/1918	28/09/1918
War Diary	Busseboom	29/09/1918	01/10/1918
War Diary	H.16.d.1.1. Sheet. 28.	02/10/1918	13/10/1918
War Diary	Sheet: 28.H.16.d.1.1.	14/10/1918	18/10/1918
War Diary	Dadizeele	20/10/1918	20/10/1918
War Diary	L.21.c.5.7.	21/10/1918	22/10/1918
War Diary	Bisseghem. Sheet 29. G29.d.3.1.	25/10/1918	26/10/1918
War Diary	G.29.d.3.1.	27/10/1918	29/10/1918
War Diary	Walle	31/10/1918	31/10/1918
War Diary	Walle. N.2c.3.0. Sheet 29.	01/11/1918	02/11/1918
War Diary	N.5c.8.8.	03/11/1918	08/11/1918
War Diary	Deerlyck. I.8.c.3.4.	10/11/1918	10/11/1918
War Diary	Vichte	11/11/1918	12/11/1918
War Diary	Berchem	14/11/1918	14/11/1918
War Diary	Nederbrakel	15/11/1918	18/11/1918
War Diary	Santbergen	22/11/1918	22/11/1918
War Diary	Grammont.	24/11/1918	13/12/1918

War Diary	Braine L'Allevd	14/12/1918	20/12/1918
War Diary	Huy: Sheet 7.	31/12/1918	31/12/1918
War Diary	Huy	01/01/1919	13/01/1919
War Diary	Cologne	21/01/1919	30/06/1919
War Diary	Kalk	01/07/1919	18/07/1919
War Diary	Kalk	19/07/1919	31/07/1919
War Diary	Marienburg	05/08/1919	29/08/1919
War Diary	Kalk	01/09/1919	29/10/1919

WO95/2630

Mar 1918 – Oct 1919

52 Mobile Veterinary Section

⑤

41ST DIVISION   FRANCE

52ND MOBILE VETY SECN.

MAY 1916 – ~~DEC 1918~~ 1917 OCT

1918 MAR – 1919 OCT

ITALY 1917 NOV – 1918 FEB

Box 2630

41

5th Mob. Vety...

Vol 22

Army Form C. 2118.

WAR DIARY
or
INTELLIGENCE SUMMARY.
(Erase heading not required.)

Sheet I.

Place	Date	Hour	Summary of Events and Information	Remarks and references to Appendices
CAMPOSAMPIERRO.	2.3.18.		Entrained locally for France. Evacuated 8 horses & 1 mule to Vety aid Post at Camposampierro	
	5.3.18.		Detrained at DOULLENS, & marched to LUCHEUX.	
	8.3.18.		Marched to LES ANVILLES farm near COUTURELLE.	
	16.3.18.		Evacuated 20 horses & mules by rail from FREVENT to ABBEVILLE.	
	21.3.18.		Evacuated 12 horses, 4 mules & 1 mule by rail from FREVENT to ABBEVILLE. Section marched to LOUVENCOURT.	
	"		March continued to HEILLY.	
	22.3.18.		Marched to ABLAINZEVELLE.	
	23.3.18.			
	24.3.18.		Marched to ACHIET-LE-PETIT, & then retired to PUISIEUX. No. S.E.6023 Pte WEEDS joined the section. One section rider strayed from advanced aid post & was lost.	

Army Form C. 2118.

WAR DIARY
or
INTELLIGENCE SUMMARY.

Sheet II.

(Erase heading not required.)

Instructions regarding War Diaries and Intelligence Summaries are contained in F. S. Regs., Part II. and the Staff Manual respectively. Title pages will be prepared in manuscript.

Place	Date	Hour	Summary of Events and Information	Remarks and references to Appendices
PUISIEUX	25.3.18.		7 horses & 1 mule destroyed. Section marched to HEBUTERNE, & then to St. AMAND.	
	26.3.18.		Section marched to camp near BAILLEULMONT. 23 horses evacuated by rail from SAULTY to ABBEVILLE.	
	28.3.18.		Evacuated 3 horses & 1 mule from QUOY-en-ARTOIS to ABBEVILLE by rail.	
	"		Section marched to GOMBREMETZ.	
	29.3.18.		4 horses & 1 mule evacuated by rail from SAULTY to ABBEVILLE. Section marched to AUTHIE.	
	30.3.18.		Evacuated 3 horses & 1 mule to 5th Corps Evacuation Station.	

J.T. Macdonald,
Capt. A.V.C.

52 Mob Vety Sec
Vol 23

WAR DIARY
INTELLIGENCE SUMMARY

Sheet I.

Place	Date	Hour	Summary of Events and Information	Remarks and references to Appendices
AUTHIE	1.4.18.		Section marched to FAMECHON. Few horses w four mules evacuated to V Corps V.E.S.	
FAMECHON	2.4.18.		Evacuated 2 horses to V. Corps. V.E.S.	
	3.4.18.		Section marched to PETIT HOUVIN.	
PETIT HOUVIN	4.4.18.		Entrained locally & detrained at PEZELHOEK. Marched from there to a farm at K.Y.c.54. Sheet. 27.	
K.Y.c.54.	7.4.18.		Section marched to farm near WATOU. K.J. d.8.7. Sheet. 27.	
K.J. d.8.7.	8.4.18.		The following men were sent to VIII Corps V.F.S. for duty. S.E.5281 Pte. Bartlett. J.W. S.E.5056 Pte. Beattie. J. S.E. 9632 Pte. Griffin. S.W. S.E.6023 Pte. Weeds. W. 28932 Pte. Dawson. H. S.E.8391 Pte. Jeffries. J.A.	

Army Form C. 2118.

WAR DIARY
or
INTELLIGENCE SUMMARY.
(Erase heading not required.)

Sheet II.

Place	Date	Hour	Summary of Events and Information	Remarks and references to Appendices
Sheet: 27. K.5.d.8.4.	9.4.18.		No. 442 Sgt. Long. B. returned from leave.	
	10.4.18.		Section marched to Camp at Sheet: 28. G.5.b.4.6. & took over from 18th M.V.S.	
Sheet: 28. G.5.b.4.6.	11.4.18.		No. S.E. 5056. Pte: Beattie. J. evacuated to 64th C.C.S.	
			10 horses & 1 mule evacuated to VIII Corps V.E.S.	
	12.4.18.		18 horses & 1 mule evacuated to VIII Corps V.E.S.	
	14.4.18.		13 horses, 3 mules & 1 hide evacuated to VIII Corps V.E.S.	
	15.4.18.		1 horse & 2 mules to II Corps V.E.S. Five privates returned from Corps V.E.S. to the section.	
	17.4.18.		1 horse evacuated to II Corps V.E.S. by float. New float obtained, old one (condemned previously by V.O.M.) returned.	
	18.4.18.		50 over troop evacuated by II Corps V.E.S. at A.28.d.9.4. Sheet 28.	

Army Form C. 2118.

WAR DIARY
or
INTELLIGENCE SUMMARY.
(Erase heading not required.)

Part III

Instructions regarding War Diaries and Intelligence Summaries are contained in F. S. Regs., Part II. and the Staff Manual respectively. Title pages will be prepared in manuscript.

Place	Date	Hour	Summary of Events and Information	Remarks and references to Appendices
A.28.d.9.d. Sheet 28.	22.4.18.		Evacuated 22 horses & 4 mules to II. Corps V.E.S. 37th M.V.S. arrived & shared our camp.	
	23.4.18.		26 kits sent to II Corps V.E.S.	
	24.4.18.		Evacuated 11 horses & 4 mules to II. Corps V.E.S. 37th M.V.S. moved out of camp.	
	25.4.18.		Evacuated 11 horses to II. Corps V.E.S.	
F.28.c.7.1. Sheet 94.	26.4.18.		Section marched to F.28.C.7.1. Sheet 29.	
	26.4.18.		Evacuated 8 horses & 1 mule to II. Corps V.E.S. No. SE 26925 Pte. MORGAN. B. joined the section from No.14 Veterinary Hospital.	
	29.4.18.		No. T4/094168. Dr. PARKES. A. (attached) was wounded. Both supply wagon horses killed by shell-fire.	
	30.4.18.		Evacuated 7 horses & 3 mules to II Corps V.E.S.	

J. Macdonald.
Capt: A.V.C.
O.C. 52nd M.V.S.

30.4.18.

Army Form C. 2118.

5"2 Mob Vety Sec

Vol 2

WAR DIARY
or
INTELLIGENCE SUMMARY.

Sheet I.

Place	Date	Hour	Summary of Events and Information	Remarks and references to Appendices
F.27.b.6.4.11. Sheet 27.	1.5.18.		Section moved to Jewellers' Camp. F.27.a.2.9. Sheet 27.	
F.27.a.2.9.	2.5.18.		Evacuated 16 horses & 3 mules to II Corps V.E.S.	
	3.5.18.		do. 8 " " 2 " " " "	
	4.5.18.		" 7 " " " " to II Corps V.E.S.	
	6.5.18.		" 5 " " " " " " (one Remount case).	
	8.5.18.		" 5 " " " " "	
	10.5.18.		" 4 " " 4 mules " " "	
	11.5.18.		" 6 " " 1 " " " "	
	13.5.18.		" 6 " " " " " " (Including 1 German horse).	
			S.S.8391 Lt Jefferies J.A. S.S.8201 Lt: Bartlett J. & A.C.28932	
			Pt Dawson H. transferred to II Corps V.E.S.	
	14.5.18.		Evacuated 6 horses & 3 mules	
			S.E.6023 Pt. Meads W. & A.C.28925 Pt. Morgan B. transferred to 22nd Corps V.E.S.	

Army Form C. 2118.

WAR DIARY
or
INTELLIGENCE SUMMARY.
(Erase heading not required.)

Instructions regarding War Diaries and Intelligence Summaries are contained in F. S. Regs., Part II. and the Staff Manual respectively. Title pages will be prepared in manuscript.

Place	Date	Hour	Summary of Events and Information	Remarks and references to Appendices
Sheet 74. F.94.a.2.9.				
	16.5.18.		Evacuated 9 horses & 9 mules to = Corps M.V.S.	
	18.5.18.		" 6 " " 1 " " = " "	
			S.E. 8395 Pte: Brown, N.S. transferred to = Corps M.V.S.	
	20.5.18.		Evacuated 4 horses, 1 mule & 2 hides to = Corps M.V.S.	
	21.5.18.		Evacuated 4 " 2 " " " "	
	22.5.18.		" 11 horses 2 " " " " (Brencourt aux).	
			Veterinary Aid Post established at A.22. E.5.5. Sheet: 28. (Cpl: Barnes & 2 men).	
	23.5.18.		Evacuated 15 horses & 9 mules.	
	24.5.18.		" 12 " " 6 "	
	25.5.18.		" 9 " " 1 "	
	27.5.18.		" 4 " " - "	
	29.5.18.		" 1 " " 3 mules.	
	30.5.18.		" 2 " " 1 mule.	

J.F. Macdonald.
Capt. A.V.C.

Army Form C. 2118.

WAR DIARY
or
INTELLIGENCE SUMMARY.
(Erase heading not required.)

5-2 Mob Vety See

Vol 26

Place	Date	Hour	Summary of Events and Information	Remarks and references to Appendices
F.27.a.29. Sheet 24.	1.6.18.		Evacuated 12 horses to 1 Cps V.C.S.	
	2.6.18.		No. 178 S.Sgt. Illingworth, O. transferred to No. 24 Veterinary Hospital. No. 85. 4664 Pte. Prior, J. granted 14 days leave to England. Veterinary Aid Post closed. Evacuated 4 horses & 1 mule to 1 Cps V.C.S.	
	3.6.18.		Section marched to ZEGGERS-CAPPEL, & halted for the night.	
	4.6.18.		Section marched to KINDERBEECK, & encamped at Q.33. d.8.3. Sheet 27.	
KINDERBEECK	6.18		Evacuated 2 horses to 23rd Veterinary Hospital.	
	8.6.18.		do. 9 " " 2 mules to 23rd Veterinary Hospital. do.	
	9.6.18.		do. 29 horses & 2 mules do. do. Inspection of Section by A.D.V.S. XII Corps.	
	10.6.18		Evacuated 27 horses & 1 mule to 23rd Veterinary Hospital.	

WAR DIARY
or
INTELLIGENCE SUMMARY.

Army Form C. 2118.

Sheet II.

Place	Date	Hour	Summary of Events and Information	Remarks and references to Appendices
KINDERBEEK	10.6.18.		No. SE. 8362 Pte Benstead. C. granted 14 days leave to England. No. SE. 10082. Pte: Sheldrake. J.M. A.V.C. attached to section as a spare driver.	
EPERLEQUES	13.6.18.		Section marched to camp near EPERLEQUES. No. 33. F.S.S. Sheet 27/A.	
			Evacuated 14 horses & 1 mule to 23rd Veterinary Hospital.	
	14.6.18		Capt. J.T. MacDonald A.V.C. leave to England.	
	15.6.18		Evacuated 2 horses & 2 mules to 23 Veterinary Hospital. Capt. F.E. Williams A.V.C. took command of section.	
	16.6.18		Evacuated 5 horses & 2 mules to 23 Veterinary Hospital.	
	19.6.18		(Including 1 mare) 3 Riders & 52 M.U.S. issued to 2 & 10th Royal West Kents. 1 to 10th Queens R.W.S.	
	20.6.18		W.S.I. 7164 Pte Prior S. returned from leave	
	22.6.18		Evacuated 10 horses & 3 Mules to 23 Veterinary hospital	

Army Form C. 2118.

WAR DIARY
or
INTELLIGENCE SUMMARY.
(Erase heading not required.)

Instructions regarding War Diaries and Intelligence Summaries are contained in F. S. Regs., Part II. and the Staff Manual respectively. Title pages will be prepared in manuscript.

Sheet 3

Place	Date	Hour	Summary of Events and Information	Remarks and references to Appendices
Eperlecques	24-4-18		Evacuated 6 horses, 6 Mules to 23 Veterinary hospital	
	25-4-18		Evacuated 2 horses to 23 Veterinary hospital. Section Marched to Zeggers Cappel & halted for 1 night.	
	26-4-18		Section Marched to Hoofde. 5A Mob. Vet. Section joined H.Q. here.	
	27-6-18		St 8383 Pte Bewshood C returned off leave	
			St 8382 Pte Bewstone C admitted to 14 F. Amb Fd Ambulance	

J.A. [signature] Captain
O.C. 5 M.V.S.

[Stamp: MOBILE VETERINARY SECTION No. 5 Date 30/4/18]

Army Form C. 2118.

WAR DIARY
or
INTELLIGENCE SUMMARY.
(Erase heading not required.)

52 Most Vety Sec

Sheet I.

Place	Date	Hour	Summary of Events and Information	Remarks and references to Appendices
Mob 50a. L.15.b.9.g.	1.7.18		Section marched to Sheet 57. K.21.d.7.3. & encamped. Capt. J.H. MacDonald returned from leave.	
Sheet 57. K.21.d.7.3.	2.7.18		Capt: J.E. Williams. A.V.C. & No. 23511.8 Pte Hacker. rejoined their unit. Evacuated four horses & one mule to II Corps V.E.S.	
	3.7.18		do. eight do. & two mules do do.	
	4.7.18		do. twelve do do do.	
			SE.6121 Cpl. Osborn W.W. granted 14 days leave to England. SS.4787 Pte. Rees R.H. attached to 9. A.H.Q.	
	5.7.18		Evacuated 13 horses & 3 mules to II Corps V.E.S.	
	6.7.18		T.T. 558945 Sgt. Wilcock A. granted 14 days leave to England.	
	8.7.18		Evacuated eight horses to II Corps V.E.S.	
	9.7.18		Evacuated five horses & two mules to II Corps V.E.S.	
	10.7.18		No. 12474 Pte. Petrie J. 1st Lost Surreys granted 14 days leave to England.	

WAR DIARY
or
INTELLIGENCE SUMMARY.

(Erase heading not required.)

Army Form C. 2118.

Sheet II

Place	Date	Hour	Summary of Events and Information	Remarks and references to Appendices
K.21.d.4.3.	10.7.18		Evacuated four horses & one mule to II Corps V.E.S.	
			No. 16350 Pte. Dawson W. admitted to 138 Field Ambulance.	
	11.7.18.		Evacuated 9 horses & 2 mules to II Corps. V.E.S.	
			No. 13824 Pte. Bishop A. granted 14 days leave to England.	
	12.7.18		Bishop A.Cpl. Section marched to Sheet 27. K.27.d.9.7. & encamped.	
K.27.d.9.7.	14.7.18.		Evacuated 9 horses & one mule to II Corps V.E.S.	
	15.7.18.		do 4 do do do do.	
	16.7.18.		do 6 do to II Corps V.E.S.	
	17.7.18.		do 3 do do do.	
	18.7.18.		do 2 horses & 2 mules to II Corps V.E.S.	
	do		No. 13819 L.S. Harbottle A.A. granted 14 days to England.	
	19.7.18.		Evacuated 3 horses & 2 mules to II Corps V.E.S.	

Army Form C. 2118.

WAR DIARY
or
INTELLIGENCE SUMMARY.

(Erase heading not required.)

Sheet III.

Instructions regarding War Diaries and Intelligence Summaries are contained in F. S. Regs., Part II and the Staff Manual respectively. Title pages will be prepared in manuscript.

Place	Date	Hour	Summary of Events and Information	Remarks and references to Appendices
K.24.d.94. Sheet 27.	20.7.18		Evacuated 6 horses & 3 mules to No. 2 V.F.S.	
	21.7.18		do 7 do & 2 do do	
	22.7.18		do 3 do to No. 2 V.F.S.	
	"		No. 7632 Pte: Griffin. S. granted 14 days leave to England	
	"		No. 6121 Corp: Osborn. N.W. returned from leave.	
	24.7.18		Evacuated 7 horses & 2 mules to No. 2 V.F.S.	
			No. 6075 Corp: Barnes. F. granted 14 days leave to England.	
	25.7.18		Evacuated 25 horses & 12 mules to No. 2 V.F.S.	
	26.7.18		do 9 " & 2 " to No. 2 V.E.L.	
	27.7.18		do 3 " & 1 mule do	
			No. TT/02345 Sgt. Wilcock. A. returned from leave.	
	28.7.18		SE. 10082 Pte: Shellorake F.W. transferred to No. 2 Vety Hospital for reclassification by medical board.	

Army Form C. 2118.

WAR DIARY
or
INTELLIGENCE SUMMARY.
(Erase heading not required.)

Sheet IV.

Place	Date	Hour	Summary of Events and Information	Remarks and references to Appendices
Sheet 27. K.24. d.9.4.	28.7.18.		S.E. 12824 Pte. Bishop. O. & 12454 Pte. Petrie J. not hitherto returned from leave. S.E. 8643 Pte. Ridley G.H. granted 14 days leave to England.	
	29.7.18.		Evacuated 4 horses & 1 mule to No. 2 V.E.S. L.E. 15953 Pte. Mitchell J. joined section as reinforcement from No. 2 Vety. Hospital.	
	30.7.18.		S.E. 15017 Pte. Irving. R. granted 14 days leave to England. Evacuated 9 horses & 1 mule to No. 2 V.E.S.	
	31.7.18.		Evacuated 1 horse & 5 mules to No. 2 V.E.S.	

J.F. Woodroofe
Capt. A.V.C.
O.C. 52 Mob. Vety. Section.

WAR DIARY
or
INTELLIGENCE SUMMARY.
Army Form C. 2118.

52 Mob. Vety. Sec.

Sheet I.

Place	Date	Hour	Summary of Events and Information	Remarks and references to Appendices
Sheet 27. K.27. C.9.1.	1.8.18.		Evacuated 4 horses & 1 mule to No. 2 V.F.S.	
	2.8.18.		" 5 " & 2 " "	
	3.8.18.		J.E. 13819. L.S. Harbottle. A.A. returned from leave. Evacuated 5 horses to No. 2 V.F.S.	
	4.8.18.		T/1094188 Dr. Watkins. S.J. granted leave to England.	
	5.8.18.		Evacuated 14 horses & 3 mules to No. 2 V.F.S. also one mule	
	6.8.18.		" 5 " " " "	
	7.8.18.		" 4 " " " "	
	8.8.18.		" 4 horses to No. 2 V.F.S.	
	9.8.18.		S8.4787 Pte. Rees. R.H. granted 14 days leave to England. S8.1632 Pte. Griffin. W. returned from leave.	
	do.		Evacuated 4 horses & 1 mule to No. 2 V.F.S.	
	do.		3 horses to No. 2 V.F.S.	
	11.8.18.		26075 Cpl. Barnes. F. returned from leave.	
	12.8.18.		Evacuated 10 horses & 4 mules to No. 2 V.F.S.	

Army Form C. 2118.

WAR DIARY
or
INTELLIGENCE SUMMARY.

(Erase heading not required.)

Sheet 11.

Instructions regarding War Diaries and Intelligence Summaries are contained in F. S. Regs., Part II. and the Staff Manual respectively. Title pages will be prepared in manuscript.

Place	Date	Hour	Summary of Events and Information	Remarks and references to Appendices
K.27.d.9.7.	13.8.18.		5 horses & 4 mules evacuated to No. 2 V.F.S.	
	14.8.18.		9 horses & 2 mules do.	
			S.E. 8643 Pte: Ridley. G.H. returned from leave.	
	15.8.18.		S.E. 15142 Pte: Hay. C.E. granted 14 days leave to England.	
			6 horses, 1 mule & 1 hide evacuated to No. 2 V.E.S.	
	16.8.18.		5 horses, 5 mules & 1 hide do.	
			S.E. 5028 Pte: Renton. J. granted 14 days leave to England.	
	17.8.18.		3 horses, 3 mules & 3 hides evacuated to No. 2 V.F.S.	
			The following Category B. men reported from No. 2 Convalescent Horse Depot for duty.	
			T.T. 03799 Pte: Booker. W.: S.E. 13699 Pte: Christy. J.	
			S.E. 14121 Pte: Browning. E: 33299 Pte: Chinnings. R.	
			27899 Pte: Aldershaw S.E. 30299 Pte: Smith. J.	
			T.T. 03417 Pte: Summerbell. E.G. 22180 Pte: Sullivan. E.R.	

WAR DIARY
or
INTELLIGENCE SUMMARY.

(Erase heading not required.)

Army Form C. 2118.

Sheet III.

Place	Date	Hour	Summary of Events and Information	Remarks and references to Appendices
K.27.d.9.4.	17.8.18.		The following N.C.O. & men left for No.2 Veterinary Hospital for medical inspection & classification.	
			L.C. 6121 Corp: Osborn. N.W. L.C. 12824 Pt: Bishop. A.J.	
			L.C. 4632 Pt: Griffin. L. L.C. 11664 Pt: Jones. J.	
			L.C. 9441 Pt: Mackenzie. A. L.C. 7664 Pt: Prior. J.	
			L.C. 8643 Pt: Ridley. G.H.	
	18.8.18.		4 horses, 3 mules & 2 hides evacuated to No. 2 V.E.S.	
			L.C. 15017 Pt: Irving. R. returned from leave.	
	19.8.18.		L.C. 15017 Pt: Irving. R. left for No. 2 Veterinary Hospital for medical examination & classification.	
			3 horses & 2 mules to No. 2 V.E.S.	
	20.8.18		Evacuated 3 horses & 3 mules to No. 2 V.E.S.	
			T.4/094188 Dr. Watkins. A.J. A.S.C. returned from leave.	

Army Form C. 2118.

WAR DIARY
or
INTELLIGENCE SUMMARY.
(Erase heading not required.)

Sheet IV.

Instructions regarding War Diaries and Intelligence Summaries are contained in F. S. Regs., Part II. and the Staff Manual respectively. Title pages will be prepared in manuscript.

Place	Date	Hour	Summary of Events and Information	Remarks and references to Appendices
K.24.d.9.7. Sheet 24.	21.8.18.		Evacuated 26 horses & 4 mules to No. 2 V.F.S. SE.5987 Pte: Watson J. granted leave to England.	
	22.8.18.		Evacuated 5 horses to No.2 V.F.S.	
	23.8.18.		do. 3 do. & 2 Mules to No.2 V.F.S.	
	24.8.18.		do. 4 do. & 3 mules do. do.	
	26.8.18.		do. 6 do. & 4 do. do. do.	
			SE.8643 W.O/P.Cpl: Ridley. G.H. & four men returned from No. 2 Veterinary Hospital classified Category B.	
	27.8.18.		SE.4787 Pte: Rees. R.H. returned from leave. Four horses evacuated to No. 2. V.F.S.	
	28.8.18.		Three horses & three mules evacuated to No. 2 V.F.S. SE.34216 Pte: Salmon G.W. SE.34596 Pte: Blundell. H. SE.98741 Pte: Crump: F. SE.34586 Pte: Reed. A. joined section from No. 4 C.H.D.	

Army Form C. 2118.

WAR DIARY
or
INTELLIGENCE SUMMARY.
(Erase heading not required.)

Sheet. V.

Instructions regarding War Diaries and Intelligence Summaries are contained in F. S. Regs., Part II. and the Staff Manual respectively. Title pages will be prepared in manuscript.

Place	Date	Hour	Summary of Events and Information	Remarks and references to Appendices
R.37.d.9.7. Sheet 27.	29.8.18.		AE. 6075 Corp: Barnes & two men sent to No. 2 Veterinary Hospital for medical examination & classification. Evacuated 2 horses to No. 2 V.E.S. Section marched to RENESCURE, - halted for one night.	
	30.8.18.		Section proceeded to WIZERNES & encamped.	
	31.8.18.		SE.17.12.d. SE.23970 Pte Wingate W. & AE.23970 Pte Bryant E. reported for duty from No.4. C.H.D.	

J. F. Macdonald
Capt.
O.C. 52 M.V.S.

[Stamp: NO. 52 MOBILE VETERINARY SECTION]

Army Form C. 2118.

WAR DIARY
or
INTELLIGENCE SUMMARY.
(Erase heading not required.)

Sheet I.

Place	Date	Hour	Summary of Events and Information	Remarks and references to Appendices
NIZERNES.	1.9.18.		4 horses & 1 mule evacuated to No. 23 Vety. Hospital.	
	2.9.18.		Section marched to ZERMEZEELE.	
	3.9.18.		Section marched to HILLHOEK area & took over from 27th American Divisional M.V.S.	
Sheet 27. 2.13.a.95.	4.9.18.		3 horses & 1 mule evacuated to No. 2 V.F.S. L/Cpl. Hay C.E. & Pte Renton J. returned from leave.	
	5.9.18.		Three horses collected at DROGLANDT & evacuated to No.2. V.F.S. S.E. 5987 Pte. Petera returned from leave.	
	6.9.18.		Lt. 141152 L/Cpl. Hay & six men sent to No.9 Veterinary Hospital Sherpenberg for medical inspection & classification, four surplus to establishment.	
	7.9.18.		Section marched to G.26.a.1.9. Sheet.28. Sh. 6095 L/cpl: Barnes. J returned to unit Category. B.1.	
	8.9.18.		Five horses & one mule evacuated to No.2 V.F.S.	

Army Form C. 2118.

WAR DIARY
or
INTELLIGENCE SUMMARY.
(Erase heading not required.)

Sheet I.

Instructions regarding War Diaries and Intelligence Summaries are contained in F. S. Regs., Part II. and the Staff Manual respectively. Title pages will be prepared in manuscript.

Place	Date	Hour	Summary of Events and Information	Remarks and references to Appendices
Sheet 28. C.26.a.	9.9.18.		Dr. Dunn. J. A.S.C. granted 14 days leave to England.	
	10.9.18.		Three horses & two mules evacuated to No. 2 V.F.S.	
	11.9.18.		6 horses & 3 mules evacuated to No. 2 V.F.S.	
	12.9.18.		Col. Stack. A.D.V.S. XIX Corps inspected section. Destroyed one H.D. 10th Middlesex.	
	13.9.18.		Evacuated 5 horses 2 mules & 4 tides to No. 2 V.F.S.	
	14.9.18.		do 3 do to No. 2 V.F.S.	
	15.9.18.		Section moved to L.28. C.2.7. Sheet 27.	
Sheet 27. L.28.a C.2.7.			returned from base. SS. 14121 Pte. Browning granted 14 days leave to England.	
	17.9.18.		Lt. 5989 Pte. Watson. J. Lt. 4664 Pte. Prior. L. to No. 2. Vety. Hospital. Evacuated 6 horses to 10th F.S.	
	18.9.18.		Evacuated 8 horses to No. 10 V.F.S. Visit of Col. F. Wilson D.V.S.	
	20.9.18.		Sgt. Long. B. granted 14 days leave to England. Australian no 2/190 R.F.A. destroyed.	
	21.9.18.		Evacuated 3 horses & 2 mules to No. 10 V.F.S.	

Army Form C. 2118.

WAR DIARY
or
INTELLIGENCE SUMMARY.
(Erase heading not required.)

Sheet III.

Instructions regarding War Diaries and Intelligence Summaries are contained in F. S. Regs., Part II. and the Staff Manual respectively. Title pages will be prepared in manuscript.

Place	Date	Hour	Summary of Events and Information	Remarks and references to Appendices
L.28.c.2.t. Sheet 28.	23.9.18.		Evacuated 2 horses & 3 mules to No. 10. V.E.S.	
	26.9.18.		Four horses evacuated to No. 7. V.E.S. Lt. Dunn J. (A.V.C.) returned from leave.	
	28.9.18.		Evacuated four horses to No. 7. V.E.S. Section marched to G.16.d.A.8. Sheet 28. near BUSSEBOOM.	
BUSSEBOOM.			Aid post established at H.13.d. central.	
	29.9.18.		Evacuated 4 horses, 7 mules & 1 hide to No. 7. V.E.S. Aid post moved to Halfebeat Corner. H.32.d.	
	30.9.18.		Evacuated 7 horses to No. 7. V.E.S One I.D. Roan mare (1st R.W. Kents) destroyed owing to shellwounds.	

J. Macdonald. Capt. A.V.C.
O.C. 32. M.V.S.

Army Form C. 2118.

WAR DIARY
or
INTELLIGENCE SUMMARY.
(Erase heading not required.)

Place	Date	Hour	Summary of Events and Information	Remarks and references to Appendices
BUSSEBOOM.	1.10.18		3 horses & two mules evacuated to No.7.V.F.S.	
H.16.d.1.1. Sheet 28.	2.10.18.		Section marched to H.16.d.1.1. & encamped.	
	3.10.18.		5 horses & one mule to No.7.V.F.S. Aid post established at O.8.a.4.7.	
	4.10.18.		7 mules to No.7.V.F.S.	
	5.10.18.		11 horses & 1 mule to No.7.V.F.S.	
	6.10.18.		6 do & 2 mules to No.7.V.F.S.	
	7.10.18.		6 horses & 2 mules to No.7.V.F.S. Aid post moved to I.10.d.7.1.	
	8.10.18.		13 horses & 9 mules to No.7.V.F.S. Capt R.L. Armour A.V.C. & two batmen attached to M.V.S.	
	9.10.18.		14 horses to No.7.V.F.S. No. 9441 Pte. MACKENZIE. A. granted 14 days leave to England.	
			No.472.Sgt.Ing.B. &6.14121 Pte Browning. returned from leave.	
	10.10.18.		3 horses, 9 mules & 2 fides to No.7.V.F.S.	
	11.10.18.		3 horses to No.7. V.F.S.	
			6 horses & 1 mule to No.7.V.F.S.	
	12.10.18.		12 horses & 4 mules to No.7.V.F.S.	
	13.10.18.		2 horses & 2 mules to No.7.V.F.S.	

Army Form C. 2118.

WAR DIARY
or
INTELLIGENCE SUMMARY.
(Erase heading not required.)

Sheet 11.

Instructions regarding War Diaries and Intelligence Summaries are contained in F. S. Regs., Part II. and the Staff Manual respectively. Title pages will be prepared in manuscript.

Place	Date	Hour	Summary of Events and Information	Remarks and references to Appendices
Sheet 28. H.16.d.1.1.	14.10.18		Capt. Armour & two batmen returned to 122 Inf. Brig:	
	15.10.18.		4 horses & 1 mule evacuated to No. 7. V.F.S.	
	16.10.18.		6 horses & 5 mules evacuated to No. 7. V.F.S.	
	17.10.18.		4 horses & 1 mule evacuated to No. 7. V.F.S.	
	18.10.18.		4 horses evacuated to No. 7. V.F.S.	
			1 horse evacuated to No. 7. V.F.S.	
			Section marched to RADIZEELE.	
RADIZEELE.				
L.21.b.57.	20.10.18.		Section marched to L.21.b.5.7. Sheet 28.	
	21.10.18.		9 horses & 5 mules evacuated to No. 7. V.F.S.	
	22.10.18.		1 horse & 1 mule evacuated to No. 7. V.F.S. Section marched to BISSEGHEM.	
BISSEGHEM. Sheet 29. G.29.d.3.1.	25.10.18.		4 horses & 5 mules evacuated to No. 7. V.F.S.	
	26.10.18.		3 horses & 3 mules evacuated to No. 7. V.F.S.	
			Visit of the D.V.S.	

Army Form C. 2118.

WAR DIARY
or
INTELLIGENCE SUMMARY.
(Erase heading not required.)

Instructions regarding War Diaries and Intelligence Summaries are contained in F. S. Regs., Part II. and the Staff Manual respectively. Title pages will be prepared in manuscript.

Sheet III.

Place	Date	Hour	Summary of Events and Information	Remarks and references to Appendices
G.29.d.31.	27.10.18.		One L.D. horse sold to & destroyed at COURTRAI abbattoir. 8 horses, 1 mule evacuated to No. 7 V.F.S.	
	28.10.18.		8 horses evacuated to No. 7 V.F.S. One horse destroyed. One L.D. mule sold to & destroyed at COURTRAI abbattoir.	
	29.10.18.		7 horses & 4 mules evacuated to No. 7 V.F.S. Section marched to HALLE. Sheet 29. N.2. £.30. Pte: Mackenzie. A. returned to section from leave.	
HALLE.	31.10.18.		2 horses & 9 mules evacuated to No. 7 V.F.S.	

J.F. Macdonald
Capt. A.V.C.
O.C.

1.11.18.

WAR DIARY
or
INTELLIGENCE SUMMARY.

Army Form C. 2118.

Sheet I.

Place	Date	Hour	Summary of Events and Information	Remarks and references to Appendices
HALLE. N.2 & 3.0. Shed 29.	1.11.18.		Evacuated 6 horses & 2 mules to No. 7 V.F.S.	
	2.11.18		Section marched to N.5. & 8.8.	
N.5. & 8.8.	3.11.18.		Evacuated 2 mules to No. 7. V.F.S.	
	4.11.18		Section marched to ST. LOUIS.	
	5.11.18.		Evacuated 4 horses to No. 7. V.F.S. One horse destroyed. (Epizootic Lymphangitis). No. 11164 Pte. Jones. J. granted 14 days leave to England.	
			One H.D. horse destroyed (totally unfit) at COURTRAI abbattoir.	
	7.11.18.		7 horses & 1 mule evacuated to No. 7. V.F.S.	
	8.11.18.		One H.D. horse destroyed.(shellwound). 8 horses & 1 mule evacuated to No. 7. V.F.S. Section marched to DEERLYCK. I.8. C.34.	
DEERLYCK. I.8. C.34.	10.11.18.		Evacuated 6 horses & 4 mules to No. 7. V.F.S. 22,180 Pte: Sullivan. E.R. granted 14 days leave to England. Section marched to VICHTE.	

Army Form C. 2118.

WAR DIARY
or
INTELLIGENCE SUMMARY.
(Erase heading not required.)

Sheet: II

Instructions regarding War Diaries and Intelligence Summaries are contained in F. S. Regs., Part II. and the Staff Manual respectively. Title pages will be prepared in manuscript.

Place	Date	Hour	Summary of Events and Information	Remarks and references to Appendices
VICHTE.	11.11.18.	11.11.18.	Hostilities ceased at 11 a.m.	
	12.11.18.		4 horses 3 mules evacuated to No.7 V.F.S. Section marched to BERCHEM.	
BERCHEM.	14.11.18.		Evacuated 4 horses to No.7 V.F.S. Section marched to NEDERBRAKEL.	
NEDERBRAKEL.	15.11.18.		P/S/Sgt. Fergn. B. reverted to private, & returned to No.2 Vety. Hospital. Pte. Booker returned from leave.	
	16.11.18.		10 horses 3 mules evacuated to No.7 V.F.S.	
SANTBERGEN	18.11.18.		Section marched to SANTBERGEN. Found tablets in the school.	
	22.11.18.		Section marched to GRAMMONT.	
GRAMMONT.	24.11.18.		S.S.11664 St/Sgt./A.V.R. returned from leave. A.L. 8281. S/A/Sgt. Ferguson. J. joined section from No.2 Vety. Hospital.	
	26.11.18		Evacuated 10 horses & 2 mules (also 6 horses & 1 mule from No.2 advanced V.F.S.) to No. 2 V.F.S.	

WAR DIARY or INTELLIGENCE SUMMARY

Army Form C. 2118.

Sheet III.

Place	Date	Hour	Summary of Events and Information	Remarks and references to Appendices
GRAMMONT.	27.11.18.		Evacuated 2 horses by float to No.2 advanced V.F.S.	
	29.11.18.		Evacuated 9 horses & 4 mules to No.2 V.F.S.	

J. F. Macdonald
Capt. A.V.C.
O.C. 52 M.V.S.

Army Form C. 2118.

WAR DIARY
or
INTELLIGENCE SUMMARY.
(Erase heading not required.)

52 Mot Vety Sec

Sheet: I.

Instructions regarding War Diaries and Intelligence Summaries are contained in F.S. Regs., Part II. and the Staff Manual respectively. Title pages will be prepared in manuscript.

Place	Date	Hour	Summary of Events and Information	Remarks and references to Appendices
GRAMMONT.	3.12.18.		One mule sold to butcher.	
	4.12.18.		One horse to X V.F.S. by float.	
	5.12.18.		17 horses & mules to X V.F.S.	No. A.6. 22180 Pte Sullivan returned from leave.
	7.12.18.		6 horses to X V.F.S. Pte. Aldenshaw admitted to hospital.	
	10.12.18.		3 horses to X V.F.S.	
	12.12.18.		Section marched to ENGHIEM.	
	13.12.18.		do. HAL.	
			do. to No.2. Vety: Hospital.	
			A.6. 6075 Cpl. Barnes. J. granted 14 days leave to England.	
			A.6. 30279 Pte. Smith. J. granted 14 days leave to England.	
BRAINE L'ALLEUD.	14.12.18.		Section marched to BRAINE L'ALLEUD.	
	15.12.18.		Section visited Waterloo.	
	17.12.18.		Section marched to MARBAIS.	
	18.12.18.		Section marched to MAZY.	

Army Form C. 2118.

WAR DIARY
or
INTELLIGENCE SUMMARY.

(Erase heading not required.)

Sheet II

Place	Date	Hour	Summary of Events and Information	Remarks and references to Appendices
HUY. Sheet 1.	19.12.18		Section marched to MARET-LA-CHAUSSÉE.	
	20.12.18		Section marched to HUY.	
	21.12.18		141121 Pte. Browning. E. granted 14 days special leave to England.	

J. Macdonald
Capt: R.A.M.C.
O.C. 52 M.V.S.

41

Army Form C. 2118.

5 2 Mob Vety Sec

Vol 3 3

WAR DIARY
or
INTELLIGENCE SUMMARY.
(Erase heading not required.)

Sheet 1.

Instructions regarding War Diaries and Intelligence Summaries are contained in F. S. Regs., Part II. and the Staff Manual respectively. Title pages will be prepared in manuscript.

Place	Date	Hour	Summary of Events and Information	Remarks and references to Appendices
H.V.Y.	1.1.19.		Evacuated 32 horses & 2 mules to No.13 Vety. Hospital, Huylatel.	
	7.1.19.		Evacuated 18 horses & 5 mules to No.13 Vety Hospital, Huylatel. Lt. 20549 Pte. Smith J. returned from leave.	
	8.1.19.		Lt. 34216 Pte. Salmon G.W. granted leave to U.K.	
	12.1.19.		Evacuated 3 horses & 1 mule to I Canadian M.V.S. Section marched to ANDENNE, & entrained.	
	13.1.19.		Section detained at NAHN, & marched to the Barracks, MARIENBURG, COLOGNE. Took over two farms from I Canadian M.V.S.	
COLOGNE.	21.1.19.		Lt. 08970 Pte. Bryant C. granted 14 days leave to U.K.	
	24.1.19.		Evacuated 15 horses to No.2 V.F.S.	
	29.1.19.		Sgt. R.V.S. No. 23741 Pte. Crump T. to be paid acting Corporal with effect from 9.3.25.	
	30.1.19.		Evacuated 7 horses & 1 mule to No.2 V.F.S. J.J. Macdonald Capt. OC 52 M.V.S.	

No. 52 MOBILE

J.J. Macdonald Capt.
OC 52 M.V.S.

Army Form C. 2118.

WAR DIARY
or
INTELLIGENCE SUMMARY.
(Erase heading not required.)

No. 34

Place	Date	Hour	Summary of Events and Information	Remarks and references to Appendices
COLOGNE	1/2/19		E.98th Inf. Bn. P.S.I. granted 14 days leave to England via Calais.	
			One O.R. posted to Machine Gun Battalion.	
			For losses for month see end Feb. C. No. 2 V.E.S.	
	8/2/19		73/9415 Pte Gunn admitted to Hosp. & Evacuated. 7/2/19	
	13/2/19		Lt 23970 Pte Hyndt to returned from leave & posted Section 6 Vice Pte Gunn	
	19/2/19		74/144972 Pte Raven O.A.S.C. posted Section 6 Vice Pte Gunn	
			34596 Pte Blundell O.H. Granted leave to England.	
			Capt. F. McDonald R.A.M.C. — do — do — do.	
	20/2/19		Evacuated by Hosp. +3 O.R.s to No. 2 V.E.S.	
	21/2/19		14664 Pte Yarley J. R.A.M.C. demobilized.	
	23/2/19		L.B.37741 L/Cpl Strump. L. R.A.M.C. admitted Hosp. & Evac. 74/144972 Pte James A.W. Granted leave to England	
	28/2/19		Evacuated of Hosp. 6 O.R.s to No. 2 V.E.S.	

for O.C. Investigat Coy
M.O. i/c 52 F.V.S.

V/T3 A.V.C.
Maj CAMC
19/9 V.S.

Army Form C. 2118.

WAR DIARY
or
INTELLIGENCE SUMMARY.

(Erase heading not required.)

Instructions regarding War Diaries and Intelligence Summaries are contained in F. S. Regs., Part II. and the Staff Manual respectively. Title pages will be prepared in manuscript.

Place	Date	Hour	Summary of Events and Information	Remarks and references to Appendices
COLOGNE	5.3.19		Evacuated 2 horses 1 mule to 2 V.F.S.	
	13.3.19		Lieutenant R. Hoyte proceeded on leave to England	
			No. 21447 Sgt. Hurlbutt J. proceeded on leave to England	
			Lieut McDonald returned from leave	
	14.3.19		24022 S/S Howell H. returned from leave	
	15.3.19		Evacuated 1 horse to F.S.	
			Evacuated 1 horse to F.P.S. to be evacuated to U.K.	
			Veterinary Officer of the American Service Division visited the station	
	17.3.19		9 horses 1 mule evacuated to No. 2 V.F.S.	
	21.3.19		7 horses " " "	
	23.3.19		No. 21998 Pt. Hearn J. joined unit from No. 5 Vety. Hospital	
	25.3.19		3 horses 3 mules evacuated to No. 6 V.F.S.	

Army Form C. 2118.

WAR DIARY
or
INTELLIGENCE SUMMARY.

(Erase heading not required.)

Instructions regarding War Diaries and Intelligence Summaries are contained in F. S. Regs., Part II. and the Staff Manual respectively. Title pages will be prepared in manuscript.

Sheet II.

Place	Date	Hour	Summary of Events and Information	Remarks and references to Appendices
COLOGNE	26.3.19.		Pt: Bishop: A.J. granted leave to England.	
	27.3.19.		Pt. Wingate: H. returned from leave.	
	28.3.19.		L/Cl. Harbottle: A.A. returned from leave.	
	29.3.19.		4 horses & 3 mules evacuated to No 6. V.F.S.	
	do.		Pte. Peters (foot loose?) granted leave to England.	
	30.3.19.		No 8643 Cpl. Ridley G.H. granted leave to England.	

J.T. Macdonald
Capt.

Army Form C. 2118.

WAR DIARY
or
INTELLIGENCE SUMMARY.
(Erase heading not required.)

Sheet 1.

April 1919
52 MVS

Place	Date	Hour	Summary of Events and Information	Remarks and references to Appendices
COLOGNE.	3.4.19.		TT. 02245 Sgt. Wilcock. R. A. returned from leave.	
	4.4.19.		Evacuated 4 horses & one mule. to No. 6. V.E.S. six privates R.A.V.C. joined the section.	
	5.5.19.		H.E. 8231 Sgt. Ferguson. J. & 9441 Pte. Mackenzie. A. & TT. 03799 Pte. Booker. demobilized.	
	8.5.19.		Ptes. Lox. V. Booth. R.S. & Crosland. H. joined section. Corp. Shiers. W.E. joined section.	
	10.5.19.		Pte. Fielding. J. joined section. Dr. Macdonald. T. returned to his unit. 126 Brig. A.F.A. Evacuated four horses & no mule.	
	12.4.19.		J.R.8. Pte. Chrystal. A. R.A.V.C. tried by F.G.C.M. & acquitted. Sgt. Kraft. R.F.A. returned to his unit. (London D.A.C.)	
	13.4.19.		A.E. 5987. Pte. Peters. J. demobilized.	

Army Form C. 2118.

WAR DIARY
or
INTELLIGENCE SUMMARY.

(Erase heading not required.)

Sheet # 1

Place	Date	Hour	Summary of Events and Information	Remarks and references to Appendices
CofoBNA	14.4.19.		128-24 Pte. Bishop. A.V. returned from leave.	
	18.4.19		2668 Pte. Spears. J. RAVC joined section.	
			Lt. 1643 Corp. Ridley. E.H. RAVC & 124474 Pte. Peters. J. RAVC returned from leave.	
	19.4.19.		731C513 Pr. Wilkinson. R. RAMC. granted leave to England.	
			Lt. S. Lt. Chrystal. A. demobilized.	
	21.4.19.		Five horses evacuated to No 6. V.F.H.	
	24.4.19.		3 horses & one mule to A.g.O. A.R.C. for Butcher.	
	26.4.19.		1389 M.Sm. Hurlsotthe.A.A. & 5T 64468 Pte. Ashton G.W. demobilized.	
	27.4.19.		2 mules & one horse sent to London B.A.R.C.	
	29.4.19.		Four Privates posted to 11 M.V.S. Northern Div.	
			Pte. Boaland granted leave to England.	

WAR DIARY
or
INTELLIGENCE SUMMARY.

Army Form C. 2118.

Place	Date	Hour	Summary of Events and Information	Remarks and references to Appendices
Cologne	29/4/19		Sheet III Command of Section taken over by Capt. W.A. Dickinson. R.A.V.C. Vice Capt. J.F. MACDONALD] R.A.V.C. Demobilized.	
	30/4/19		Evacuated. 6 Horses & 2 Mules. 6 + J.A.V.C. Gd. HINCHCLIFFE. L. Granted 14 days Special Leave.	

W.A. Dickinson
Capt R.A.V.C.
O.C. 62 M.V.S.

Army Form C. 2118.

HQ MVS / Mar 1919

WAR DIARY
or
INTELLIGENCE SUMMARY.
(Erase heading not required.)

Sheet 1.

Instructions regarding War Diaries and Intelligence Summaries are contained in F.S. Regs., Part II. and the Staff Manual respectively. Title pages will be prepared in manuscript.

Place	Date	Hour	Summary of Events and Information	Remarks and references to Appendices
Cologne	30/4/19		Evacuated to L.H.A.R.C. 6 Horses & 2 Mules	
	1/5/19		Dr. Hinchcliffe L. granted 14 Days Special leave	
			A.D.V.S. Corps inspected Unit & Bicycle Cards	
	2/5/19		23609 S.Smith Gauntlett B. joined Section for Duty	
	3/5/19		Evacuated to L.H.A.R.C. 2 Horses & 2 Mules	
	4/5/19			
	5/5/19		Section Marched to L.H.A.R.C. Kalk & took over Billets	
	6/5/19			
	7/5/19		Section Marched to Allermann Schools	
	8/5/19			
	9/5/19		Sgt Wilcock A. Departed for Demobilization	
	10/5/19		Sgt Welsh G. } Departed for Demobilization	
			Sgt Spence }	
			Sgt Seago J.C.	

Army Form C. 2118.

WAR DIARY
or
INTELLIGENCE SUMMARY.
(Erase heading not required.)

Instructions regarding War Diaries and Intelligence Summaries are contained in F. S. Regs., Part II. and the Staff Manual respectively. Title pages will be prepared in manuscript.

Place	Date	Hour	Summary of Events and Information	Remarks and references to Appendices
Cologne.	11/5/19		Col. Swan returned from leave & Posted to 6 V.E.S. for Duty	
	12/5/19		Q.M. Fox V.C. granted 14 Days leave to U.K.	
	13/5/19		A.D.V.S. Corps inspected Unit Register Cards	
	14/5/19		Evacuated to No. 8 Vety Hospital 7 Horses & 4 Mules	
	15/5/19			
	16/5/19			
	17/5/19			
	18/5/19			
	19/5/19			
	20/5/19			
	21/5/19		Evacuated to No. 8 Vety Hospital 10 Horses & 5 Mules	
	22/5/19		Evacuated to L.H.A.R.C. 2 Horses	
	23/5/19			
	24/5/19			
	25/5/19		O/C Swan granted 14 Days leave to U.K.	
	26/5/19		Q.M. Bishop Departed for Demobilization	
	27/5/19		Q.M. Fox V.C. Retd from Leave	

Army Form C. 2118.

WAR DIARY
or
INTELLIGENCE SUMMARY.
(Erase heading not required.)

Instructions regarding War Diaries and Intelligence Summaries are contained in F. S. Regs., Part II. and the Staff Manual respectively. Title pages will be prepared in manuscript.

Sheet III

Place	Date	Hour	Summary of Events and Information	Remarks and references to Appendices
Cologne	28/5/19		Pte Hinchcliffe ReTd from leave	
	29/5/19		Pte Palmer H. Granted 14 Days leave to UK	
	30/5/19			
	31/5/19		I.A.D.V.S. Inspected Section	

J. Hodgin
Capt A.V.C
O/c 52 M.V.S.

No. 52
Date 9/6/19
MOBILE VETERINARY SECTION

(A7092) Wt W12899/M1293 75,000 1/17 D D & L. Ltd. Forms/C2118/4.

Army Form C. 2118.

52. MVS

WAR DIARY
or
INTELLIGENCE SUMMARY.
(Erase heading not required.)

Instructions regarding War Diaries and Intelligence Summaries are contained in F. S. Regs., Part II. and the Staff Manual respectively. Title pages will be prepared in manuscript.

Place	Date	Hour	Summary of Events and Information	Remarks and references to Appendices
	1/6/19		Evacuated 4 Horses & 1 Mule to 32 V. Vety Hospital	
	2/6/19			
	3/6/19			
	4/6/19		A.T.V.S. Inspected Unit Reported VAD's V Section	
	5/6/19		A/T Thorneycroft R.H. Stein & Boulton Reg reported M.V.S. for Duty	
	6/6/19		III V.S. Inspected Section	
	7/6/19			
	8/6/19		Cpl Buckley & R.A.V.C. Held from Leave	
	9/6/19			
	10/6/19		Evacuated sick Horses & 19 Mules to Horse S Mules M.V.S. for Duty	
	11/6/19		368765 - Horses & 235 Employ Coy held from Leave	
	12/6/19			
	13/6/19		T128815 Pte Holmes & R.A.V.C. Held from Leave	
	14/6/19			
	15/6/19			
	16/6/19		Evacuated 17 Horses & 3 Mules to N.N.B. Vety Hospital	
	17/6/19		Cpl Sullivan R.A.V.C. RVO from Leave	
	18/6/19		Sgt Smith . . Granted 14 Days leave to U.K.	

Army Form C. 2118.

WAR DIARY
or
INTELLIGENCE SUMMARY.
(Erase heading not required.)

Sheet II

Instructions regarding War Diaries and Intelligence Summaries are contained in F. S. Regs., Part II. and the Staff Manual respectively. Title pages will be prepared in manuscript.

Place	Date	Hour	Summary of Events and Information	Remarks and references to Appendices
Cologne	19/4/19		M.V.S. Marched to Volberg	
			O/C Lieutenant F. Pursoff M.E. Cooper N.P. 23 Brother Regt	
			2nd A. Solway A.D. Ransley J. Josaphra D. Sutton A. 7 Spur Regt	
	19/4/19		Lygg. Cpls N3 7 Brother Regt —	Vety Hosp
	20/4/19		W/S Recommend W.H. S Bkn Brother Regt	No 2
	23/4/19		Foster G. 19 Brother Regt	Vety Hosp
	27/4/19		Section Marched to Overath	No 2
	30/4/19			
	22/4/19		A.T.V.S. Vaulted Section	
	24/4/19			
	25/4/19			
	28/4/19			
	29/4/19			
	30/4/19		Evacuated 5 Horses to H.S. Vety Hospital	
	30/4/19		Section Marched to Albermann Schools Wath	

W H Hughes
Capt R.A.V.C.

Army Form C. 2118.

52 MVS

WAR DIARY
or
INTELLIGENCE SUMMARY.
(Erase heading not required.)

Sheet 1

Instructions regarding War Diaries and Intelligence Summaries are contained in F. S. Regs., Part II. and the Staff Manual respectively. Title pages will be prepared in manuscript.

Place	Date	Hour	Summary of Events and Information	Remarks and references to Appendices
Holt	1/7/19			
	2/7/19			
	3/7/19			
	4/7/19		Dr Dawes A.S.C Returned to Unit. Dr Coveney joined M.V.S for Duty. Dr Bates, Dr Rowe, Dr Salway, Ramsey, Simmons, Dawsey, Bridewell Rgt joined Cooper N.H., Dammerall W.H., Musgestrial W., Sutton A., Foster G.} M.V.S. for Duty	
	5/7/19		Evacuated four horses & three mules to No 6 V.E.S	
	6/7/19			
	7/7/19		L/Sgt Rackley posted to 187 Bde H.Q for Duty	
	8/7/19			
	9/7/19			
	10/7/19			
	11/7/19		Evacuated 4 Horses & 5 Mules to No 6 V.E.S	
	12/7/19		L/Cpl Smith J Returned from Leave	
	13/7/19			
	14/7/19		Dr Bryant C granted 14 days leave to UK. Ballard A., Dr Patterson A Returned to 24 Vety Hospital Painter H., Ayres H.H. R.A.V.C joined M.V.S. for Duty	
	15/7/19			
	16/7/19			
	17/7/19			
	18/7/19		L/Cpl Kerridge W Returned from Leave	

Army Form C. 2118.

WAR DIARY
or
INTELLIGENCE SUMMARY.
(Erase heading not required.)

Sheet II

Instructions regarding War Diaries and Intelligence Summaries are contained in F. S. Regs., Part II. and the Staff Manual respectively. Title pages will be prepared in manuscript.

Place	Date	Hour	Summary of Events and Information	Remarks and references to Appendices
Aldr	19/7/19		S/Sgt Crump granted 14 Days leave to U.K.	
	20/7/19			
	21/7/19			
	22/7/19		A.D.V.S. Inspected Unit Register Cards	
	23/7/19		Evacuated 2 Horses & 3 Mules to No 6 V.E.S	
	24/7/19		Evacuated 2 Horses to No 6 V.E.S. Pte Broadfoot returned to 24 Vety Hospital	
	25/7/19			
	26/7/19			
	27/7/19			
	28/7/19		Pte Smith T.J joined M.V.S for duty	
			Pte Sutton A.J granted 14 Days leave to England 28/7/19 to 11/8/19	
	29/7/19		Evacuated 2 Horses & 1 Mule to No 6 V.E.S.	
	30/7/19			
	31/7/19		D/T Cooper granted 14 Days leave to U.K. 31/7/19 to 13/8/19	

Army Form C. 2118.

WAR DIARY
or
INTELLIGENCE SUMMARY.
(Erase heading not required.)

Instructions regarding War Diaries and Intelligence Summaries are contained in F. S. Regs., Part II. and the Staff Manual respectively. Title pages will be prepared in manuscript.

Sheet 1

Place	Date	Hour	Summary of Events and Information	Remarks and references to Appendices
Field	1/7/19			
	2/7/19			
	3/7/19			
	4/7/19		D. Davies A.S.C Reinvid to Unit. N Downey Joined M.V.S for Duty 2/Lt Daws & Rouse 9th Res Regt Solvene, Hanley, Johnson, Simmons, Passey & Dawes Rgt amp began H.A Dammeral H.A Assistant H. Sutton A, Foster 9 M.V.S. for Duty Evacuated 800 horses & 9802 spells to F.G. V.E.S	
	5/7/19			
	6/7/19			
	7/7/19		2/Lt Frickley posted to 187 Bn H.G. for Duty	
	8/7/19			
	9/7/19			
	10/7/19		Evacuated 4 Horses & 5 spells to 92.6 V.E.S	
	11/7/19		L/Cpl Smith Returned from Leave	
	12/7/19			
	13/7/19			
	14/7/19		2/Lt Bryant C Granted 14 Days Leave to UK Bollard A, pte Patterson A Returned to 24 Very Hospital Painter YH, - Agnes H.H R.A.V.C Joined M.V.S for Duty	
	15/7/19			
	16/7/19			
	17/7/19			
	18/7/19		9/Cpl Kewidge H Returned from Leave	

Army Form C. 2118.

WAR DIARY
or
INTELLIGENCE SUMMARY.
(Erase heading not required.)

Sheet II

Place	Date	Hour	Summary of Events and Information	Remarks and references to Appendices
Halr	19/7/19			
	20/7/19		2/Sgt Crump granted 14 Days Leave to U.K.	
	21/7/19			
	22/7/19			
	23/7/19		A.D.V.S Inspected Unit Register Cards	
	24/7/19		Evacuated 2 Horses & 3 Mules to No 6 V.E.S	
	25/7/19		Evacuated 2 Horses to No 6 V.E.S. Pte Broadfoot returned to 34 Vety Hospital	
	26/7/19			
	27/7/19			
	28/7/19		Pte Smith H. Joined 14.V.S for duty. Cpl Sexton A. Granted 14 Days Leave to England 28/7/19 to 11/8/19	
	29/7/19		Evacuated 2 Horses & 1 Mule to No 6 V.E.S.	
	30/7/19			
	31/7/19		D/S Cooper Granted 14 Days Leave to U.K. 31/7/19 to 13/8/19	

1/8/19

[signature] Capt
R.A.V.C.

Army Form C. 2118.

WAR DIARY
or
INTELLIGENCE SUMMARY.
(Erase heading not required.)

No 52 MVS

Place	Date	Hour	Summary of Events and Information	Remarks and references to Appendices
MARIENBURG	5/8/19		Visited 52 M.V.S. - Unit A8 of Signals	
	6/8/19		" " " DAROS	
			" - Mgr. E Hearne Royal Hdqs has told 8.7.14.22.64	
	11/8/19		Classification of animals of DA8 of Signals	
	13/8/19		Visited 52 M.V.S. - Unit A8 of Signals	
	22/8/19		Inspected following Units viz. ADVS L/Corps - Signals - 11th Queens - 2/4 Queens - C/pp Rdr	
			5/pp - 23rd Middlesex	
	25.8.19		Capt Body joined for duty as o/c DAROS	
	26.8.19		Attended animals of D48 of Signals	
	27.8.19		Visited 52 M.V.S. - DA8 of Signals	
			ADVS 6th Corps	
	28/8/19			
	29.8.19		M.V.S. - Attended animals of D.A8 and M.G.B.P	

B.Body
Capt R.A.V.C.
o/c ADVS
Lieutenant

Army Form C. 2118.

WAR DIARY
or
INTELLIGENCE SUMMARY.
(Erase heading not required)

Instructions regarding War Diaries and Intelligence Summaries are contained in F. S. Regs., Part II. and the Staff Manual respectively. Title pages will be prepared in manuscript.

Place	Date	Hour	Summary of Events and Information	Remarks and references to Appendices
Kalk	1		—	
	2		—	
	3		—	
	4		—	
	5		—	
	6		Evacuated to No 6 V.E.S. 6 Horses + 1 mule	
	7		Evacuated to No 8 Vety Dot. 7 Horses	
	8		—	
	9		Evacuated to 6 V.E.S. 4 Horses + 1 mule	
	10		R.A.V.C. Grants No 498 Vety Dot 1 mule	
	11		Pte Farrer W Simpson Middlesex Regt 14 days leave to U.K.	
	12		A.D.V.S. Inspects Infantry with attached M.V.S.	
	13		Pte Sutton Middlesex Regt Rtn from leave. Pte Barritt R.A.V.C. 24th Vety Hosp	
	14		Joined M.V.S. per draft. Evacuated to No 8 Vety Hosp Dot 1 Horse.	
	15		Genl Butler Inspects M.V.S. Section	
	16		Pte Bennett R.A.V.C. Grants 14 days leave to U.K. 19/8/19 to 2/9/19	
	17		—	
	18		Evacuated 3 Horses + 11 mules to No 706 V.E.S.	
	19		A.D.V.S. Inspects Walers of 1 Vety Chgd of Remts	
	20		Pte Murloypha D____ Middlesex Grants 14 days leave to U.K.	
	21		Evacuated 3 Horses + 1 mule to No 6 V.E.S.	
	22		—	
	23		Evacuated 1 Horse + 4 mules to No 6 V.E.S.	
	24		—	
	25		Pte Pagsley of Simpson 23rd Middlesex Rtn from leave Pte Blundell R.A.V.C. Rtn from leave	
	26		Pte Pagsley of Simpson Grants 14 days leave to U.K. Pte Pansby of Simmons 23rd Middlesex	
	27		Grants 14 days leave to U.K.	
	28		Evacuated to No 8 Vety Dot 1 mule 5 Horses + 1 mule to 6 V.E.S.	
	29		—	
	30		10th Palan R.A.V.C. demobilised	
	31		—	

J.J. Joseph (Capt R.A.V.C.)

Army Form C. 2118.

WAR DIARY
or
INTELLIGENCE SUMMARY.

(Erase heading not required.)

Instructions regarding War Diaries and Intelligence Summaries are contained in F. S. Regs., Part II. and the Staff Manual respectively. Title pages will be prepared in manuscript.

Place	Date	Hour	Summary of Events and Information	Remarks and references to Appendices
Kalk.	1st			
	2		—	
	3		—	
	4		—	
	5		Evacuated to 6 VES 6 Horses & 1 Mule	
	6		—	
	7		Evacuated to 8 Vety Detach 1 Horse	
	8		—	
	9		—	
	10		Evacuated to 6 VES 4 Horses & 1 mule ⟨illeg⟩ 8 Vety Detch 1 Mule	
	11		17th Bn and RAVC Grants 14 days Leave to UK	
	11		17th Pantry & Simmons + Middlesex Reg Grants 14 days leave to UK	
	12		A.D.V.S. Inspects Infantry Horses attached M.V.S.	
	13		17th Butler (Middlesex) & 35th Puddick from Leave. 17th Barritt R.A.V.C. 24th Vety Hosp	
	14		Joined MVS for Duty. Evacuated to 4308 Vety Hosp Qrs 1 Horse	
	15		Lieut Butler Inspects M.V.S. Section	
	16		17th Osmond of R.A.V.C. Grants 14 days leave to UK 19/3/5 to 2/4/5	
	17		Evacuated 3 Horses & 1 Mule to No 6 VES	
	18		ADVS Inspects Tablets of Vety Chest Oof Lieut. 17th Gangahia 1 Middlesex Grants 14 days	
	19		Evacuated 3 Horses & 1 mule to No 6 VES	
	20		Leave to UK	
	21		Evacuated 7 Horses & 4 mules to No 6 VES	
	22		17th Pantry & Simmons 23rd Middlesex Returns from Leave. 17th Plumptree RAVC Rtd from Leave	
	23		South Dunlop Grants 14 days Leave to UK. 17th Partry & Simmons 23rd Middlesex Rptd to Unit	
	24		Evacuated to No 8 Vety Detach 1 mule. Evacuated to No 6 VES 5 Horses & 1 mule	
	25		17th Palmer RAVC Rejoined M.V.S.	
	26			
	27			
	28			
	29			
	30			
	31			

Hodge Capt RAVC

Army Form C. 2118.

WAR DIARY
or
INTELLIGENCE SUMMARY.
(Erase heading not required.)

Instructions regarding War Diaries and Intelligence Summaries are contained in F. S. Regs., Part II. and the Staff Manual respectively. Title pages will be prepared in manuscript.

Place	Date	Hour	Summary of Events and Information	Remarks and references to Appendices
KANK	Sept. 1949			
	1		5811/15 taken over by Capt 96 stair RAMC from Cay Hodgson RAMC	
	2		Arrived to #1 C.C.S. returned 2 mules	
	3		1724 Cpl Hardick R. RAMC Despatched to reinforce Corps Field Amb	
			22223 Pte Dennett " returned from leave	
	5		Evacuated to 1 F.C.C.S. Barnard 4 mules	
	6		" " " 4 mules	
	7		8643 Sgt Roder L.G. RAMC Evacuated 4 days sick to 1 F.A.	
	8		1733 L.Cpl Ponsonby R " " " despatched to Battalion Corps Field Amb	
			2280 L.Cpl Childress E.B "	
	11		Strafed by McYes Sullivan Shrapnel wound L. hand L. Leg	
	12		– T20053 L/Cpl Rhodes RASC wounded in knee	
			At Sullivan	
			Case to be Jews 23.9.19 – 23809 Pte Gaunch E. RAMC returned from leave	
	13		16347 Cp Marshall II 1st Welsh Regt returned from leave	
	14		" " to his Unit	
	15		Capt Roylaic RAMC Three days 21 days leave to U.K	
	17		Corpt L/P Richards & Neme & L Connors L/P 20 days Leave	

Army Form C. 2118.

WAR DIARY
or
INTELLIGENCE SUMMARY.
(Erase heading not required.)

Place	Date	Hour	Summary of Events and Information	Remarks and references to Appendices
KALK	18		Evacuated to N°6 V.E.S. 1 horse	
	20		" " 2 horses + 1 mule - Evacuated to N° Stationary 1 horse	
	23		" " 2 horses + 1 mule	
			" " " 1 horse	
	24		34193 Sgt Ridley E.M. admitted to 1st base	
			The following men despatched to Rawalpindi: 28411 Spr Burgoyne 3316 bombardier	
			23609 f Grewton E.g 23970 Pte Bryant C.E. 19606 Pte Goderch R.H. 19791 Pte Smith W. 19508 Pte Smith D.	
			30279 Pte Smith J.	
	25		Evacuated to N°8 Bristchish Officers - Sgt F. Smith admitted Camp 1 horse	
	26		" N°6 V.E.S. 2 horses " N°24 Vc despatched to Rawalpindi	

Maj RAVE
7 OC 52 M.V.S.
London Div

Original

Army Form C. 2118.

No. 52nd Mobile Veterinary Section
London Division

WAR DIARY
or
INTELLIGENCE SUMMARY.
(Erase heading not required.)

Place	Date	Hour	Summary of Events and Information	Remarks and references to Appendices
KALK	9/10/18		Evacuated 2 horses to No 6 V.E.S.	
	3/10/18		Evacuated 1 horse to No 2 V. Hospital & 6 horses & 1 mule to No 6 V.E.S.	
	4		" " "	
	7		" " Mules	
	9		" " 1 h.o.s. Veterinary hosp. Transport & 4 horses	
	10		" " 2 horses to No 6 V.E.S.	
			Sick Transferred Remount Camp	
	11		1 Pony died & 1 mule 3 Mgs Alfo Base R=A to U.K 14/10/18 3/11/18	
	12		Evacuated 2 H.2.3 wounded during to No 6 V.E.S.	
	13		" " Remount Camp	
			Evacuated 1 horse w/ mule to Southern Remount Camp No 1 V.E.S.	
	14		1 " " w/ Riding horse & Lt w/unded 2 horses sick	
			& 14 light draft wounded 1 horse to No 6 V.E.S. Evacuated 1 mule to 6 C.R.P.	
	15		7 sick & 5 wounded horses 1 mule to No 6 C.R.P.	

Army Form C. 2118.

WAR DIARY
or
INTELLIGENCE SUMMARY.
(Erase heading not required.)

Instructions regarding War Diaries and Intelligence Summaries are contained in F. S. Regs., Part II. and the Staff Manual respectively. Title pages will be prepared in manuscript.

Place	Date	Hour	Summary of Events and Information	Remarks and references to Appendices
K.E.K.	22/10/19		Capt. Shepherd R.F.V. or Bakmar (Pte C Shepherd 28 R.F.) evacuated to take charge during absence of Capt Stewart on leave	
	23/10/19		Evacuated 6 Russians 3 males to No 8 Vety Hospital Pte Eagar T.M. SE11246 am Pte Kellet T SE26956, Pte Rose E SE 21846 R.M.C. arrived here from 21 M.T.S. (Transport under reorganisation for shift)	
	26/10/19		Capt. J. E. Stenn R.F.C. % arrived from U.K. & taken up of Board	
	27/10/19		Evacuated # Horse to No 8 Vety Hospital Col Willis (SE 3826) evacuated from No 8 Vety Hospital under supervision of Rose (Pony)	
	28/10/19		Cpl Bell G.A. SE 467 R.A.S.C. arrived from No 11 M.T.S. in accordance with E.D.V.C. orders for instruction to drive R.A.C. Dvr Marsh SK 576, Paddington P. SE 4600 Rd Page Lt SE 22676 R.A.S.C. Pte Peberdy R SE 26798 arrived from No 11 M.T.S. on duty with L.A.D.V.C. Indian C.of F.	
	29/10/19		Pte Turner H L 29583 R.A.C. returned from leave to U.K.	
	29/10/19		Sgt Jackson R 85H R.H.& S.B.R. R.A.O (R.S.V.) posted to 184 Bde R.F.A + Sgt Proctor A.B. 49704 R.M.C to 52nd Mobile Vety Sections + Sgt hollow Turner	

www.ingramcontent.com/pod-product-compliance
Lightning Source LLC
Chambersburg PA
CBHW081244170426

43191CB00034B/2035